Narrative, Nature, and the 'Cock' and 'Bull' Story:

The Lockean *Tristram Shandy* and the Modern Novel

By
Amanda Tiller,
B.A.(Hons), M.A., M.L.I.S

Narrative, Nature, and the 'Cock' and 'Bull' Story: The Lockean *Tristram Shandy* and the Modern Novel

This literary work is protected under copyright laws in Canada, the United States, and elsewhere internationally.

No part of this book shall be reproduced or transmitted in any form or by any means, electronic or mechanical, including photocopying, recording, or by any information retrieval system without written permission of the publisher.

Although every precaution has been taken in the preparation of this book, the publisher and editor assume no responsibility for errors or omissions. Neither is any liability assumed for damages resulting from the use of this information contained herein.

Copyright © 2006, 2013. All rights reserved.

ISBN-13: 978-0-9869027-9-6

Published by Problematic Press.

To purchase copies of this book, please visit:
http://problematicpress.wordpress.com

Printed in the United States.

Cover image: *The Effects of Trim's Eloquence* by By George Cruikshank (1792–1878) [Public domain], via Wikimedia Commons.

The hat logo is a trademark of Problematic Press.

For Dad.

Abstract

The Life and Opinions of Tristram Shandy, Gentleman (1760) is a complex and challenging read due to the many deviations, tangents and time lapses uncharacteristic of contemporary prose works. This analysis explores the evolution of the novel, the traditional form and structure of the novel, and the impact of the originality and uniqueness of Sterne's *Tristram Shandy* on the literary medium as an art form, at the time of publication. This paper will explore reactions, reviews, revere, and outrage which erupted from a neo-classically-minded literary milieu, rooted in the traditional rules of the ancients, including those defined by Aristotle in his profoundly influential *Poetics* (330 BCE), a treatise which would become a universal guideline for dramatic composition, as well as for the style of multiple literary genres. Sterne was one of the first to stray. Although he does not imitate nature in the way that Aristotle intended, however, Tristram's very effort to tell his life story in an original and uninfluenced way leads him to a more precise imitation of nature than perhaps, adherence to these guidelines could have procured. I have endeavored to explore the inherent nature in Tristram's narrative with reference to John Locke's *An Essay Concerning Human Understanding* (c. 1690).

Acknowledgements

This publication was originally written as a research paper or short dissertation required for the fulfillment of my Master of Arts degree in English, Language and Literature at Memorial University of Newfoundland. I completed the degree in the Fall semester (September) of 2006, and recently endeavored to revisit the work in an attempt to edit and revise for publication. The original work could not have been completed without the support, guidance, and feedback of my dissertation supervisor, Dr. Don Nichol, whose unparalleled knowledge, scholarship, and patience, motivated and equipped me to mould and organize my thoughts and insights. My thanks is also extended to Dr. Danine Farquharson, who provided a second reading and feedback to further guide the outcome of this work, and also to the many faculty members at Memorial University's Department of English, Language and Literature, who fostered and supported my love of English literature.

Of course, my thanks would not be complete without acknowledging the love and support of my friends and family at the time of original composition. I would also like to thank those who have encouraged me to edit this dissertation, in recent years, for publication: firstly, my friend Dave Reynolds, founder and owner of, and publisher for, *Problematic Press*, who told me to "go for it," and encouraged me to get my research and scholarship out there. To Stephanie Ayers, who seconded Dave's recommendation, to Nicholas Morine and Jessica Walsh, who advised, encouraged, and provided me with an example upon which to grow and strive. To Marie Murphy, who makes me see the beauty and possibility in all things, to Shalon and Jason Noble, my greatest influences, to Andy Fowler, my confidant and supporter in every conceivable way, to Shannon, Sue, my sister Krista and brother-in-law, Jeff, and to so many other amazing, accomplished, and strong people in my life, who inspire me to challenge myself, I thank you.

Most importantly, thank you, a million times over, to my heroes, my Mom and Dad. You both showed me the meaning of strength, endurance, happiness, acceptance, hard work, and dedication. You gave me the unfailing confidence and support I needed to accomplish everything I have wanted to accomplish in life. You gave freely of yourselves, your experiences, your hearts, your lives, and your love, and you did so selflessly and profoundly, and I love you both more than words could ever express. I would be nothing at all without the love with which you both have showered me my entire life. I hope I have made you proud; that has been my primary goal. Mom, I love you endlessly, and look forward to the new life upon which we are embarking, together. Dad...I love you, and I miss you. You were my best friend, and I dedicate everything I am, everything I will ever be, and everything I will ever do, to your precious memory.

Contents

Abstract..4

Acknowledgements..5

Introduction:
Tristram Shandy, Precursor to the Modern Novel
....10

Chapter 1:
Classical Literature/ Neo-Classical Literature:
Transcending the Aristotelian Unities..............13

Chapter 2:
Sterne and the Sentimental Novel....................16

Chapter 3:
Sterne in Context......................................19

Chapter 4:
Sentiment and Sensibility.............................25

Chapter 5:
Tradis-tram; a New Tradition.........................29

Chapter 6:
Locke's Essay, and Sterne's Public: Critical
Reception..34

Chapter 7:
Un-Locke-ing the Mind: Shandean Associations
and Derivations..38

Chapter 8:
Truth and Nature/ Nature and Truth..................50

Chapter 9:
And so it Be-ends...56

Conclusion:
The Story of a "Cock and a Bull…"....................59

Appendix..64

Works Cited...66

Introduction:

Tristram Shandy, Precursor to the Modern Novel

Laurence Sterne's *Life and Opinions of Tristram Shandy, Gentleman* was hailed by many critics, including Samuel Johnson and Samuel Richardson, upon the publication of its first two volumes in 1760 as a work not to be taken seriously by the literary public. Nonetheless, *Tristram Shandy* is recognized today as a precursor to the modern novel. Writing, in part, for financial gain and literary recognition, Sterne was profoundly influenced by the fashionable and non-traditional style of the sentimental novel which had previously procured, for such authors as Henry Fielding, a substantial fortune. Also writing in the tradition of the sentimental novel, Sterne was influenced by the textual innovations of such authors as Samuel Richardson and John Kidgell, whose visual deviations including pictorial representations and skewed script, are mirrored throughout the text of *Tristram Shandy*. Despite its obvious influences, however, *Tristram Shandy* was often defined by such critics as Edmund Burke as an original text, a claim refuted by the original artisans of Sterne's style, including Richardson. Along with his adherence to the stylistics of the sentimental tradition, Sterne too, is an opponent of classical authority, a definitive aspect of the form. Where Sterne differs, however, and where his contribution to the evolution of the novel lies, is in his unique concentration on the mind.

Aristotle dictates in his *Poetics* (330 BCE), the necessary conformity to a unified plot in works of tragedy, as well as the elements which contribute to a sound imitation of nature. Until the publication of works which include *Tristram Shandy*, these Aristotelian standards maintained their strong-hold within the literary and, in particular, the dramatic community; the conformity to a unified plot, as seen in the non-dramatic works leading up to and including those produced in Sterne's time, however, suggest that Aristotle's influence, indeed, transcended literary genres. Viewing these traditional literary rules, however, as the source of contemporary literary limitation and unoriginality, Sterne redirects his focus away from literary expectation and onto the self, thus, onto his personal objectives for the novel. For this, Sterne turns to John Locke, and gains inspiration for his novel from Locke's *Essay Concerning Human Understanding* (c. 1690), whose theories regarding cognition and the truths inherent in the association of ideas, mirror the deviations, incongruity, and apparent nonsensicality of *Tristram Shandy*. Tristram, as the novel's subjective narrator, allows his mind to control the work, and as a reflection of his mind, *Tristram Shandy* can be viewed as a satirical mapping of the Lockean consciousness. Throughout the narrative, Tristram struggles to complete the story of his birth, though his thoughts do not allow him to chronologically leave Shandy Hall on the day of his arrival. Through his willing surrender to the mind's natural digressions, Tristram does, in fact, discover the Lockean truths which lie within himself. Expecting every day to be his last, Tristram realizes that as his life-story can never achieve Aristotelian completion, neither can his life. The mind, consisting of endless associations, will never stop associating. Thus, in reality, the unified plot is impossible and, despite Aristotelian doctrine, does not reflect nature. Life, like his story, he realizes, is merely the story of "A COCK and a BULL" (IX, xxxiii, 809), or, a series of unplanned events, unrealized intentions, and haphazard misfortunes. Here, the Aristotelian unities fall short. If a story is to imitate nature, it cannot attain closure; Thus, dispelling Aristotelian claims to natural imitation, a story which imitates nature cannot be unified into a distinctive beginning, middle and end. *Tristram Shandy* does not simply reject tradition, however, it frames the rejection of tradition in the contemporary preference of mind over intellect, proving that the mind is the true representation of nature, and displacing the authority that had, thus far, prevailed for centuries.

Chapter 1:

Classical Literature/ Neo-Classical Literature: Transcending the Aristotelian Unities

In the years leading up to the mid-eighteenth-century, otherwise known as the early neo-classical period, classical literary theory prevailed, defining and determining the mechanical structure of the English novel. It was the common opinion during the seventeenth and much of the eighteenth-centuries, Irène Simon notes in *Neo-Classical Criticism: 1600-1800*, that literature was to comply with "specific rules which all craftsmen must know if they are to ply their trade properly." These rules were to be derived from the theories of the ancients, whose "works had stood the test of time" (12). The universal regard for the genius of ancient literature, however, is not the only reason for its lasting reputation. According to Simon, the ancients not only created timelessly beautiful texts, but truthful texts as well, imitating perfectly, the realities of nature. It is because of this timeless quality that early neo-classicists were expected to imitate the very essence of classical literature in order to secure literary immortality, as well. Thus, a true poet "should learn from those who had imitated nature. Such alone were the ancients...[who] mirror nature and appeal to what is common to all men, not to the taste of a particular time or place" (12). These sentiments are reiterated by Samuel Johnson who, in *The Rambler*, mirrors the conventional belief that fiction should strive to "'represent...life in its true state,' present[ing] 'portraits of which everyone knows the original, and can detect any deviation from exactness of resemblance'." Moreover, the novel should, if in accordance with these laws, "'distinguish those parts of nature which are most proper for imitation'" (19). Of the ancient influences, Aristotle's methods as outlined in the *Poetics*, serve as the neo-classical guidebook for proper literary composition.

According to Aristotle, the *Poetics* detail "the correct way to construct plots if the composition is to be of high quality." The essential criteria for this standard of literature are, essentially, unity and the proper imitation of nature. Plot must be presented as a "whole," meaning "that which has a beginning, a middle, and an end." Thus, as Aristotle concludes, "well-constructed plots should therefore not begin or end at any arbitrary point, but should employ the stated forms" (13-14). In terms of imitation, Aristotle defines the perfect plot as the "imitation," not "of persons, but of actions and of life." Moreover, this imitation should represent "complete...whole, actions, possessing a certain magnitude" (11-13). For Aristotle, the correct imitation of nature, or, of life, entails the completion representative of the unified plot.

These guidelines were followed from the beginning of the seventeenth and into the mid-eighteenth-century. In fact, as Michael Macrone notes in *It's Greek to Me!*, "until about the late eighteenth-century, it was generally agreed that the educated person ought to be equipped with a basic knowledge of ancient languages, and be liberally read in key works by Aristotle, Cicero, Virgil and Plutarch" (xii). It was following this period, however, that various "essential" unities dictated by Aristotle began to crumble, a pattern most profoundly evident in the eighteenth-century sentimental novel.

Chapter 2:

Sterne and the Sentimental Novel

The sentimental novel, although reflecting in many respects, characteristics of classical literature, became defined as such in the eighteenth-century by the literary mode which sought to deconstruct ancient definitions of sentimentality and unity. Although recognized as a popular literary form in the eighteenth century, Laura Jane Ress, in her work, *Tender Consciousness*, insists that "the sentimental novel was...not invented" during this period. It is but an evolved version of a traditional genre "recurring through literature," and "appealing to the emotional sensibility" (63). Ress notes various examples of such past sentimental works as *King Lear*, evident in the grieving father's remorse for the demise of his loyal daughter Cordelia, and the "pastoral episodes" of *Don Quixote.* Possibly the most definitive example of a classical sentimental work, however, is *Oedipus Rex*, specifically, the climactic scene which depicts Oedipus' realization of his incestuous actions, and the shame and guilt which ensues (63). Yet, a distinct change is evident in the sentimental works of the eighteenth century. Whereas traditional sentimental literature centers, as Ress suggests, on "emotional release," the eighteenth-century sentimental novel depicts profound displays of "sympathy" (63). The abundant display of sentimentality characteristic of the genre, or, as Leo Braudy, author of *The Form of the Sentimental Novel* defines, the "inarticulate language of the heart," serves not only to uniquely situate it within the sentimental tradition, but also to reject classical norms, in that the "inarticulate language" which defines the form, results in the inarticulate structure of the novel, though in complete opposition to Aristotelian unitary ideals:

> Introspection has specific effects on the sentimental novel's focus... [and because] contemplation opposes intuition to rationality, and leaves sentimental writers unsure of being able to fully express private experience... the authors cannot force structural or chronological closure. (Ress 65)

Thus, the eighteenth-century sentimental novel tends not to uphold the Aristotelian unities required in the years previous. Braudy further insists that the genre "rejects the older shapes of intellectual self-consciousness as well as any formal literary sophistications authenticated by tradition" (6). What sets this form aside in the eighteenth century is its never-before-seen "oppos[ition of] intuition to rationality; [its]

disjuncture... and effusion to continuity and plot" (12). The natural result of such ancient abandonment, of course, is the "incompletion" characteristic of the form, an incompletion which Aristotle reserves for his main taboo (12). In Aristotelian philosophy, these "simple" or "episodic" plots, constitute the "worst" kinds of plots, and are simply "unacceptable" (17). Sterne, following in this tradition, imitates the dejointed and fragmented plot, as well as the many typographical elements prevalent within the sentimental tradition, in part, to gain renown through the conformity to current literary fashion.

Chapter 3:

Sterne in Context

Laurence Sterne, born of parents Roger and Agnes Sterne on November 24, 1713, as Ian Campbell Ross notes in *Laurence Sterne: A Life*, in "the small wool-town of Clonmel in County Tipperary, Ireland" (20), was well into his forty-sixth year before he experienced literary fame with the publication of *Tristram Shandy*. A former "country parson," Sterne was "unaffectedly delighted by the sudden shift in his fortunes. He had long sought to escape the predictable and uncongenial rural existence to which his modest income and still more modest prospects had restricted him" (Ross 1). To do this, Sterne constructed his most successful work, *Tristram Shandy*, in accordance with the unconventional structure of the contemporary sentimental novel, the current literary fashion. Although, as Arthur H. Cash notes in *Laurence Sterne: The Early and Middle Years*, that "there is no certain evidence of [Sterne's] reading of the novels of Richardson, Fielding or Smollett...we can hardly doubt he did so" (199). Sterne's intentions for *Tristram Shandy* most prominently reflect those of Henry Fielding, who like Sterne, "need[ed] to make a living" and as such "became a prolific writer of comedies and farces," or, contemporary literary fashion (Gardiner 315). Ross, who cites Fielding's notion that "'Fashion'" is the "'Governor of this World'," also insists that it is this compliance to literary fashion which largely defines Fielding's influence on the work of Sterne, whose "fashion," has "brought [him] hitherto undreamt-of opportunities" (8). Published in serial format, *Tristram Shandy* granted Sterne financial security until his death in 1768, just "fourteen months" after "the appearance of the ninth volume" of his work (New 831). The main influences for Sterne's style, however, can be accredited to such sentimental authors as Richardson, who inspired many of the textual oddities which, in part, defined the sentimental fashion.

Upon its publication, *Tristram Shandy*[1] was often accredited with textual uniqueness, incorporating elements and devices never before seen in the English novel. At first glance, it is clear that *Tristram Shandy* is an unusual text owing to randomly-situated blank, blackened, and marbled pages, its empty and incomplete

---

[1] Citing, *The Florida Edition of the Works of Laurence Sterne: 'The Life and Opinions of Tristram Shandy, Gentleman. Vol. I-III'* Ed. Melvyn New and Joan New. Gainesville: UP of Florida, 1978, a definitive edition inclusive of the original manuscript of *Tristram Shandy*, as well as extensive notes, both authorial and editorial.

chapters, as well as its grammatical and stylistic oddities. Upon the introduction of widow Wadman, for example, Tristram provides for the reader, an empty space upon which he can describe the widow as he himself "fanc[ies]" her (VI, xxxviii, 566). Blackened pages are given upon the announcement of the death of Yorick (I, xii, 37-8), as well as marbled pages (III, xxxvi, 269-70), which, as Thomas Keymer notes in *Sterne, the Moderns, and the Novel*, reflect the disorder and chaos inherent in the text (80). The presence of empty chapters is noted in volume IV, when Tristram decides that chapters xviii and xix would best be described elsewhere, following chapter xxv (IX, 770-90). In addition, the text's grammatical and stylistic oddities including excessive dashes and asterisks, contribute to the obvious visual unconventionality of the novel (VI, xvii-xviii, 524-29). These many textual absurdities were recognized by such critics as Edmund Burke, who, despite his clearly communicated dissatisfaction with the novel as a whole, commends Sterne for his originality, resolving that "the faults of an original work are always pardoned." Burke also admits that it is "not surprising, that at a time, when a tame imitation makes almost the whole merit of so many books, so happy an attempt at novelty should have been so well received" (qtd. in Anderson 481). Just as Burke relishes the originality of *Tristram Shandy*, and its uninfluenced nature so, too, does Samuel Johnson acknowledge this originality in his prediction that "nothing odd will do long" (qtd. in Anderson 484). Modern criticism exhibits the same recognition of Sterne's originality, as Duncan Campbell notes about the novel in *The Beautiful Oblique*:

> It is regarded as being of primary importance —in its dismantling of narrative conventions, its foregrounding of the act of writing, its direct address to the reader, its fracturing of chronological order and its typographical experimentation...[and finally] as a precursor of (post) modern literary technique. (11)

Tristram Shandy, however, does not fully adhere to these claims of originality. In mechanical terms, the novel is not original to itself, but original to the form of the contemporary sentimental novel. Keymer notes the many influences which combine to form the text of *Tristram Shandy*, acknowledging the presence of many "elements of Sterne's earlier style," which contained traditional "Scriblerian echoes and tricks," combined with "elements astutely geared to modern metropolitan taste, including satirical play on the latest novelistic conventions and knowing allusions to current bestsellers" (2). Many of these techniques and, in particular, Sterne's textual devices, are characteristic of the sentimental novel, harkening back, as Keymer notes, to such works as Richardson's *Clarissa*, in which the author toys with the conventions of textual structure, "skewing" various portions of the text throughout the margins (50). As Braudy notes, this "scattering of sentences about the page" is a visual representation of Clarissa's "distraught frame of mind," and the resulting "distraction" between thought processes. Moreover, Braudy suggests that it is "from such tentative seeds [that] ...Sterne's more elaborate formal disruptions in *Tristram Shandy*" spring forth" (10). Sterne not only had Richardson's intentions in mind upon the composition of *Tristram Shandy*, but as Keymer notes, the intentions of William Owen and John Kidgell, as well.

As in the example of Richardson, Sterne is not the first to make wide use of the asterisk as an indication of "whispered," interrupted, or inaudible speech. Owen, however, in his comparatively unsuccessful, but influential work, *The Life and Memoirs of Mr. Ephraim Tristram Bates*, which preceded *Tristram Shandy* by almost five years, holds that honour (67). Lastly, Keymer cites John Kidgell as another of Sterne's great influences in terms of textuality. The influence of Kidgell's *The Card* is evident in Sterne's work, in its similar use of illustrations planted randomly throughout the text, adhering quite literally, to the eighteenth-century belief that "images are more easily conceived than described" (77). Reminiscent of Sterne's illustrative "flourish" (IX, iv, 743), and visual depictions of the non-sequential progress of his novel (VI, xl, 570-71), Kidgell inserts, as well, the depiction of a "ten of clubs," fore grounded by a letter (Appendix). All texts are precursors to *Tristram Shandy*, yet all contain the unique elements often accredited to this later work. In addition to its typographical influences, however, Sterne himself also admits, despite his insistence in *Tristram Shandy* that "I shall confine myself neither to [Horace's] rules, nor to any man's rules that ever lived" (I, iv, 5), that he has indeed been influenced by "Cervantic humour," in a letter "To a Friend" (qtd. in Anderson 462). Similarly, in a letter to Jane Fenton, Anderson notes Sterne's confession that his novel is filled with "laughable humour,— with equal degree of Cervantik satyr" (465). While addressing his sentimental influences, however, and while maintaining certain traditional fashions of the sentimental novel, Sterne redirects the emphasis, in *Tristram Shandy*, from the sentimental language of the heart to the cognitive construct of the mind.

Chapter 4:

Sentiment and Sensibility

"Sensibility" is defined by Stephen Brumwell and W. A. Speck in *Cassell's Companion to Eighteenth-Century Britain* as "the notion of innate sympathy for the suffering of others, which developed from moral philosophy in the eighteenth century." Sympathy in the novelistic form was indicative of the eighteenth century and many of the writers who thrived during the period. One of these writers was Samuel Richardson, who "played like a virtuoso on the sympathies of his readers by portraying virtue in distress in his heroines Pamela and Clarissa." Richardson's work, without a doubt, embodied the essence of the sentimental novel, and despite Sterne's liberty in imitating many of Richardson's techniques, "such emotions" were not celebrated in the works of Sterne so much as they were "exploited to excess." In Sterne's *A Sentimental Journey* (1768), for example, the author "manipulates" sensibility, essentially mocking the contemporary trend, "to the point of indulging in sorrow, not just out of sympathy for victims...but for its own sake" (345). A similar trend is evident in *Tristram Shandy* in Tristram's empathy for uncle Toby. As in *A Sentimental Journey*, Sterne translates Tristram's empathy for Toby into a sorrowful lament:

> Alas! 'twill exasperate thy symptoms, –check thy perspirations,–evaporate thy spirits... ring thee into a costive habit of body, impair thy health,–and hasten all the infirmaties of thy old age. –O my uncle! My uncle *Toby*. (II, iii, 104)

Throughout the text, the extreme release of sorrow is prominent; however, the conventional novel is also mocked by Sterne's work, in its comical presentation of despair, or, in its "gentle mock[ing of] mawkishness because it signals an abandonment of reason" (Ress 77). In relation to Tristram's misfortunes, Walter asks Toby, "did ever a poor unfortunate man, brother Toby... receive so many lashes?" Mocking his brother's self-pity and dramatic attitude, Toby responds, "The most [lashes] I ever saw given...(ringing the bell at the bed's head for Trim) was to a grandier, I think, in Makay's regiment." Evidently, Toby does not care for Walter's moanings, having witnessed real pain, and also having experienced a potentially mortal injury at the battle of Namur (I, xxi, 75). In response to Toby's non-chalance, Walter is stunned, and "had my uncle *Toby* shot a bullet thro' my father's heart, he could not have fallen down with his nose upon the quilt more suddenly" (IV, iii, 328). Walter may request sympathy, but sympathy cannot be granted from one who deems it to be undeserving.

Similar apprehension to sorrow is evident in the reaction of Walter to Trim's recollections of his brother Tom. Upon remembering "poor *Tom*!...tortured upon a rack for nothing," Trim weeps uncontrollably, "pulling out his handkerchief," and wails, "these are misfortunes...worth lying down and crying over." In response, Walter "could not help blushing," and when Trim suddenly "brighten[s] up...My father," replies Tristram, "could not help smiling." Then, as quickly as his spirits lift, they plummet once more after Toby's generous assurance of lifelong financial security. As a sign of gratitude, and in his "attempt...to thank my uncle *Toby*," Tristram reveals how Trim "had not [the] power" to do so, "tears trickl[ing] down his cheeks faster than he could wipe them off." Again, Tristram notes, "My Father smiled" (IV, iv, 329-30). Here, as in *A Sentimental Journey*, characters exhibit exaggerated sorrow, mocking the genre which fosters it. In addition, Walter's casual grin reveals his inner mockery of Trim's relentless sniveling. As Brumwell and Speck note, the Shandean novel which exudes despair "for its own sake," will not be accommodated with a sympathetic response, especially in the work of an author who deems such excess to be laughable. Clearly, as the act of extreme emotion tires, so too does the convention. Sterne aims to communicate the need for change in the sentimental novel by satirizing the hilarity of its current intentions. Ress notes:

> In writing *Tristram Shandy* [Sterne's] head ultimately rules his heart...the situations or characters' responses may display natural sensibility, but sheer emotion does not determine Sterne's presentation; at that point in his writing career, he did not subscribe to the cultish exaggerations of Sentimentalism. (77)

Unconventionally, Sterne moves the focus of his work from the heart to the head, and from emotion to the mind. As Sterne steers the novelistic convention away from sentimentality through this redirected focus, he gently leads it into its next and most lasting stage of development with the help of the revolutionary cognitive theories of John Locke. Aided by these theories, Sterne creates a new order independent of Aristotelian unities, introducing the novel ordered, instead, on the natural and non-sequential progressions of human thought, and the association of ideas.

Chapter 5:

Tradis-tram; a New Tradition

Although in agreement that the English novel was in need of reformation, it is evident that the sentimental tradition was not yet willing, until the release of *Tristram Shandy*, to completely abandon traditional ties to Aristotelian unities. Despite efforts of the form to enact this liberation from the past, it is clear that the traditional "rule" of the unified plot is maintained in an effort to stabilize the novel's integrity. Braudy notes that although the sentimental novel "consider[s] the earlier forms of art an unnatural order from which they must escape...it does not totally reject all tradition, but always retains some for backdrop for the novel" (11). Even in the wake of conventional abandonment, "Richardson," for example, "rather than the refilling of a pre-existent form... was still involved in the problem of telling a complete story. At one level he wants the reader to be sure how all the characters wind up." Thus, Richardson, though a sentimental novelist, is not prepared to abandon traditional rules of narration (12). At this point, classical authority has not been completely dissolved. This all changes, however, in the character of Tristram Shandy, whose work is governed only by the natural ordering process of his own mind, signifying the evolving notion, Michael McKeon notes in *The Origins of the English Novel: 1600-1740*, that "truth" is inherent, not in traditional order, but in the "senses" (127). Tristram's surrender to his mind leads him to truths which would otherwise have gone unnoticed.

In the recording of his narrative, Tristram is influenced by nothing which does not exist in the composition of his own mind, and in this, he is unyielding. In defining the intentions of his novel, Tristram states, "I write to instruct," further revealing, "It is a history-book, Sir...of what passes in a man's own mind" (II, ii, 98). As such, he alone will dictate the telling of his story, imploring that his readers "let me go on, and tell my story my own way" (I, vi, 9). Moreover, the control which Tristram takes over the telling of his own narrative, he clearly reveals, is consciously in the absence of classical, as well as contemporary authority. On many occasions, Tristram openly "def[ies]" ancient authority and the fact that "so many playwrights, and opificers of chit chat have ever since been working upon" the minds and literary standards of contemporary audiences, including that of "*Trim*'s and my uncle *Toby*'s pattern.—I care not what *Aristotle*, or *Pacuvius*, or *Bossu*, or *Ricaboni* say," and bravely, Tristram admits, "I never read one of them," a bold statement during a time when ancient doctrine was still very much the expectation (III, xxiv, 246). Tristram is aware of and addresses this expectation, which is existent in much of his reading audience. However, he forewarns that although he is aware of the fact that "there are readers in the world, as well as many other good people in it...who find themselves ill at ease, unless they are let into the whole secret first to last," thus, in a linear fashion, "of everything that concerns you," that he has a different plan for his narrative, one which does not comply with such convention. Although, as Tristram admits, "right glad I am, that I have begun the history of myself in the way I have done; and that I am able to go on tracing everything in it, as Horace says, *ab Ovo*," or, "from the egg," or, birth, he is also quick to clarify that "in writing what I have set about, I shall confine myself neither to his rules, not to any man's rules that ever lived" (I, iv, 5). Here, it is evident that Sterne is including in this equation, the rules of his critical public, and in a display of disgust over the limitations which ancient convention has placed on society, Tristram says of his contemporaries:

> Their heads, Sir, are stuck so full of rules and compasses, and have that eternal propensity to apply them upon all occasions, that a work of genius had better go to the devil at once, than stand to be prick'd and tortured to death by 'em. (III, xii, 213)

Ancient convention has made the reading public

blind to alternate narrative possibilities, and as such, Tristram establishes his intentions to base his novel primarily on his own rules, stating, "And what of this new book the whole world makes such a rout about?...I had my rule and compasses, &c. my Lord, in my pocket.–Excellent critic!" (III, xii, 213). Later, Tristram also expresses disgust at the imitator, or, the author who bases his creation not on his own standards, but on those who predeceased him, and continue to dictate the design of his text. On this matter, Tristram "wish[es] from my soul, that every imitator in *Great Britain*, *France*, and *Ireland*, had the farcy for his pains; and that there was a good farcical house, large enough to hold...and sublimate them...all together" (V, i, 408). Not only are ancient rules limiting, but those who conform to these rules are securing their position of authority. The only way to assure complete literary independence, and enact the future of the novel free from ancient authority, is for every writer to follow his own design, and leave behind the rules inscribed by a bygone era. It is also evident that through Tristram's narrative, which he writes, in part, "to instruct" (II, ii, 98), he wishes, as well, to lead this transition away from the past and into the future, to reveal alternate possibilities for the written word. Although he realizes that the style of his text will seem abnormal and possibly distasteful to the contemporary reader, he implores them to "have a little patience" so that they may become "familiar" with each other, and that through an enhanced "knowledge" of himself, that they gain an enhanced appreciation for the story, as well, "and as we jog on, either laugh with me, or at me, or in short, do any thing,–only keep your temper" (I, vi, 9-10). If the reader is able to do this then, hopefully, he will receive the message which Sterne is attempting to deliver, namely, "that it may be a lesson to the world, '*to let people tell their stories their own way*'" (IX, xxv, 785). It is this message directed by Sterne to the general public, which has afforded him a prominent place in the evolution of the novel into its modern form.

Such later writers as Virginia Woolf applauded Sterne for such an accomplishment, insisting that "no young writer could have dared to take such liberties with grammar and syntax and sense and propriety and the long-standing tradition of how a novel should be written" (78). It is because of this change initiated by Sterne, that *Tristram Shandy* is often regarded "as a work in which the groaning conventions of mid-eighteenth-century fiction meet their parodic waterloo" (Keymer 21), and most importantly, as an influence and "precursor of [such] moderns," Watt notes, as "Proust, Joyce, and Virginia Woolf" herself (304). Tristram, as the construct and representation of Sterne, and the unique views held by Sterne in the area of authorial influence and originality, gains his insight and basis for his opinions on the work of John Locke, whose theories on ideas, association, and uninfluenced narration, inform the text of *Tristram Shandy*.

Chapter 6:

Locke's *Essay*, and Sterne's Public: Critical Reception

Anticipating Sterne's novel, Locke foregrounds his influential work, *An Essay Concerning Human Understanding*, on the idea of narrative freedom and the processes of individual thought. Before he begins the text of his lengthy cognitive theories, Locke establishes, in the *Epistle to the Reader*, the basis of his work, namely, his concern with conventional bonds, advising his readers not to allow themselves to be limited by such expectations:

> He who has raised himself above the Alms-Basket, and not content to live lazily on scraps of begg'd Opinions, sets his own Thoughts on work, to find and allow Truth, will...not miss the Hunter's satisfaction; every moment of his pursuit, will reward his pains with some Delight; and he will have Reason to think his time not ill-spent, even when he can not much boast of any great acquisition. (6)

Foreshadowing Sterne, also, is Locke's

impatience with the traditional public who fosters such stagnant convention. Defending the efforts of those who seek to break these bonds, Locke suggests, "the imputation of Novelty, is a terrible charge amongst those, who judge of Men's Heads...by the Fashions and they can allow none to be right, but the received Doctrines." He later criticizes that as a result of this conventionality, "new Opinions are always suspected and usually opposed, without any other reason, but because they are not already common." Moreover, although these new literary alternatives "be not yet current by the publick stamp; yet it may, for all that, be as old as Nature, and is certainly not the less genuine" (4). Such was the reception of Sterne's work, and while certain critics applauded Sterne's ingenuity, other readers were less than enthused. In a review of *Tristram Shandy* by Edmund Burke, for example, he protests that "the author perpetually digresses; or rather having no determined end in view, he runs from object to object." Moreover, "these digressions [are] so frequently repeated, [that] instead of relieving the reader, [they] become at length tiresome. The book is a perpetual series of disappointments" (qtd. in Anderson 481). Probably the most notoriously harsh reaction to *Tristram Shandy*, however, comes from novelist Samuel Richardson:

> In this foolish town, we are obliged to read every foolish book that fashion renders prevalent in conversation; and I am horribly out of humour with the present taste...

> Perhaps some polite person in London, may have forced this piece into your hands, but give it not a place in your library; let not *Tristram Shandy* be ranked among the well chosen authors there. (482)

Specifically, Richardson expresses a discontent with the book's "unaccountable wildness; whimsical digressions; comical incoherencies; [and] uncommon indecencies...as no decent mind can endure without extreme disgust" (483). Keymer believes, however, that Richardson's disapproval of the novel is due not to Sterne's use of digressions and "indecencies," but to the credit he received, following the publication of the novel, for the narrative techniques which Richardson, himself, believed was of his own doing, and not Sterne's. Keymer suggests that "Perhaps [Richardson] detected a strain of parody in Sterne that seemed to implicate his own techniques" (1). Nonetheless, it is evident that Sterne rejects all opinions but his own in the writing of his work, and in this Lockean mindset, he discovers the "truths" described by Sterne that can only be found through the association of his own ideas and experiences.

Sterne craved for the literary expression of the self. Similar to Locke, he strived to communicate the notion of ancient limitation and attempted, through his writing, to demonstrate to the literary public, how they have been shackled by the conventions which have, thus far, dictated the style of their literature. As Watt notes, Sterne "had read Locke, was at home with his conceptions, [and] never ceased praising him" (25). Aided by the theories of Locke, Sterne presents his characters as individuals, whose lives have been governed, and their personalities and actions molded, by the association of often unrelated ideas. In addition, Sterne's Lockean analysis allows him to achieve narrative liberation, when, in succumbing to the disorder of the mind, over the conventional order of plot, "the Aristotelian priority of plot over character [becomes] wholly reversed, and a new type of formal structure...evolve[s] in which the plot attempts only to embody the ordinary processes of life," specifically, the individual life and experiences of Tristram Shandy (Watt 292). Reminiscent of Locke, Sterne, "let[s] loose [his] own Thoughts, and follow[s] them in writing" (Locke 6). The Lockean implications in *Tristram Shandy* are undeniable, and just as Locke's treatise is "spun out of my own coarse Thoughts" (Locke 8), *Tristram Shandy*, in essence, charts an autobiographical path with Tristram's mind in the lead, and the man in tow, creating a new order of narration, and breaking the bonds of traditional obligation.

Chapter 7:

Un-*Locke*-ing the Mind: Shandean Associations and Derivations

In Sterne's novel, the lives of the Shandys are controlled, and become continually disrupted by ideas and by the association of thoughts. According to Locke, one way through which the mind unites ideas is through the pairing of those associations which are related in terms of either their pleasurable or painful connotations. Locke defines the process through which feelings of pleasure reawaken past pleasurable experiences and similarly, how feelings of pain reawaken past painful experiences. Moreover, it is these memories or ideas "which," Locke notes, "naturally at first make the deepest and most lasting Impression"; thus, "those, which are accompanied with Pleasure or Pain" (150). Elizabeth Shandy and her association of intercourse with the winding of the clock is one such pleasurable association. Because Walter Shandy "was one of the most regular men in everything he did," the sexual relations of himself and his wife are scheduled precisely "on the first *Sunday night* of every month throughout the whole year." Upon each of these Sundays, Walter has developed the habit of winding a clock before the event (I, iv, 6). Because the winding of the clock is associated, in Elizabeth's mind, with notions of the sexual pleasure which is to come, the mere act of the winding arouses her before sexual activity is even initiated:

> From an unhappy association of ideas which have no connection in nature, it so fell out at length that my poor mother could never hear the said clock wound up,——but the thoughts of some other things unavoidably popped into her head. (I, iv, 7)

Although the idea of sexual intercourse and of clock winding may seem unrelated, in a very Pavlovian way, they become associated in the mind as related events having, in the past, occurred in relation to one another. Although "Ideas," Locke states, often "are not at all of kin, [they] come to be so united in some Men's Minds," such that "'tis very hard to separate them, [because] they always keep in company, and the one no sooner at any time comes into the understanding but its Associate appears with it." For Elizabeth, the winding of the clock is unavoidably associated with sex, Walter having established the connection, and conditioning Elizabeth to do so, as well. Elizabeth's ability to "trace these [ideas], and hold them together in that Union," is owing, Locke insists, to "the office and Excellency of...Reason" (395). Experience and conditioning tells her that the two events are related.

Painful associations are also, however, accompanied in the mind, and can become united, as well, by seemingly opposing forces. Possibly the best example of painful associations in *Tristram Shandy* is in the event of Trim's recitation of the sermon, when, during a discussion of "*Religion...Mercy...*and *Justice*," he associates the "prisons of the inquisition" with his brother Tom. Although both ideas seem unrelated, Trim later explains that the "tortures" of which he is reciting are set in "*Portugal*, where my poor brother *Tom* is." Although the listeners cannot understand the connection Trim is making between the two, insisting that, "'tis not an historical account,—'Tis only a description," Trim cannot continue with the sermon, declaring, "I would not read another line of it, quoth Trim, for all this world" (II, xvii, 161-62). This occurrence illustrates Locke's definition of "Relation," whereby "the Mind so considers one thing, that it does, as it were, bring it to, and set it by another, and carry its view from one to t'other" (319). Moreover, when the mind becomes focused on this one related idea, "all the rest of our Faculties are in a great measure Useless" (153), thus, Trim's inability to read the sermon which associates for him, feelings of pain.

Many of the more comical associations are those of Walter Shandy, however, whose many eccentricities can be explained by associated ideas. Upon hearing the word "weakness," for example, Tristram explains how the very idea "struck full upon his brain, ⸺so sure it set him upon running divisions upon how many kinds of weaknesses there were;⸺that there was such a thing as weakness of the body,⸺as well as weakness of the mind" (I, xvi, 48). This incident is reminiscent of Locke's theory of memory retention, which refers to the natural process of the mind whereby those ideas which have been "imprinted" on the memory, can once again be revived. Furthermore, "it is, by the Assistance of this Faculty, that we are said to have all those Ideas in our Understandings; which though we do not actually contemplate, yet we can bring in sight, and make appear again, and be the objects of our Thoughts" (149-50). These ideas, or "little subjects of disquietude [were] springing out of this one affair all fretting successively in [Walter's] mind," as well (I, xvi, 49). Because ideas, along with all retained associations "float in our Minds," Walter's mind chooses, through a process of selection, all those ideas which coincide with his current thought, namely, the notion of "weakness," redirecting his focus successively from one related idea to another. This association of ideas is defined by Locke as the process of "attention" (Locke 227). More precisely, Walter's associative tendency is evident throughout the text, in matters mostly relating to the future and well-being of Tristram.

Walter's eccentricities defined by the

association of ideas in his mind are concerned with the establishment of his son's future success. Walter believes that this happiness is based, in part, on the "strength" of one's "Christian name." Similarly, he equates success with the length of his son's nose, as well as the character of his tutor. Tristram often discusses the absurdity of his father's notions, and in relation to his ideas on naming, Tristram explains, "his opinion...was, That there was a strange kind of magick bias, which good or bad names, as he called them, irresistibly impressed upon our characters and conduct" (I, xix, 57-8). Walter associates great men with great names, and believes that, in being given the name of a great man, one will grow to aspire to greatness, as well (58). Thus, Walter wishes to name his future son "Trismegistus," explaining to Toby, "*Trismegistus*...was the greatest of all earthly beings—he was the greatest king...lawgiver... philosopher...[and] priest" (IV, xi, 339). Certainly, one of such virtue would inspire greatness in his son. If, on the other hand, a child is in possession of a weak name, he is doomed to fail. The weakest of these names, ironically, is "Tristram," for which, "of all the names in the universe, [Walter] had the lowest and most unconquerable aversion...thinking it could possibly produce nothing in *rerum naturâ*, but what was extremely mean and pitiful" (I, xix, 62-3). Upon the accidental naming of his son, this most detestable of names, Walter displays the sorrows of a man whose son is doomed to a life of misery: "Unhappy *Tristram*! child of wrath! child of decrepitude! interruption! mistake! and discontent!" (IV, xix, 354). In addition to his damnable name, Tristram's nose, broken at birth by Dr. Slop's "vile instrument" (III, xxvii, 253), is also, according to Walter, a source for his son's eternal misfortune.

Like Christian names, Walter also associates long noses with greatness, and short ones with failure, as Tristram explains, "for three generations at least, this tenet in favour of long noses had gradually been taking root in our family," a tenet which had culminated in Walter, who "did not conceive how the greatest family in *England* could stand it out against an uninterrupted succession of six or seven short noses" (III, xxxiii, 261). Walter blames many past Shandy misfortunes on the inferior length of his grandfather's nose, from which "blow," as Tristram describes, the family "had never recovered" (261). Unfortunately, Tristram, in Walter's eyes, is the next of the Shandean cursed, screaming, "Fool, coxcomb, puppy—give him but a NOSE...[while] the door of Fortune stands open" (IV, xix, 355). Lastly, Walter associates habits and mannerisms with character, insisting, upon the selection of Tristram's tutor, that "there is a certain mien and motion of the body and all its parts, both in acting and speaking, which argues a man well within." Among them, "cheerful[ness], faceté, jovial[ity]...pruden[ce], [and] attentive[ness] to business." Among the indicators of an unfavourable character, are one who "lisp[s], squint[s]...grind[s] his teeth, or speak[s] through his nose" (VI, v, 497-8). These associations define the order of Walter's life, as well as the system of belief upon which he bases his life as well as that of his family.

Inadvertent associations are also evident in Toby, who whistles "*Lillabullero*" to dull the resonance of each unwelcome thought or opinion, or, as Tristram says, "when anything shocked or surprised him;–but especially when any thing, which he deem'd very absurd, was offer'd" (I, xxi, 78). Thus, when Trim comments upon Toby's wound and implies the sexual implications of the wound, Toby inherently begins to whistle, masking the sound of a thought of which he cares not to be reminded: "The knee," Trim begins, "is such a distance from the main body—whereas the groin...is upon the very *curtin* of the *place*," at which point, Toby "gave a long whistle," indicating his desire to change or avoid the subject (IX, xxxi, 803). As well, Toby blushes at the very mention of aunt Dinah (I, xxi, 76), and has adopted warfare as his hobby-horse, or passion, after having lost his sexual desire during his wounding in the Battle of Namur (I, xxi, 75). Associating the loss of his sexuality with warfare, Toby adopts warfare as his sexual substitute. Locke's theories of associative thoughts apply, however, not only to the novel's secondary characters, but also, and most importantly, to Tristram, whose associations present themselves more so in a textual manner.

Tristram Shandy is, quite literally, a string of associations linked one after another from beginning to end. Often, these associations lead to the flashbacks and foreshadowing, commonly termed "digressions," although more accurately termed "associations," being, in fact, ideas associated and derived from this main storyline. Manfred Pfister, in his biography *Laurence Sterne*, charts the progression of *Tristram Shandy*, illuminating the extensive detours and deviations which seem to stray from the logical progression of events in the text. To offer the most significant event, Tristram's birth, although a seemingly short recollection, it is one which takes the author four volumes, and almost three years to complete, in Sterne's time, owing to the extensive deviations or associations made along the path to completion (52-5). These associations seem to impede upon the story, related by the author who cannot seem to focus on the main event at hand. It seems odd that the simple telling of one's birth could lead to such digressions as the detailed stories of Parson Yorick and the midwife (I, vii-xvii, 10-49), the details of his parents' relationship (I, iv-xviii, 6-57), both sexual and otherwise, the unusual notions of Walter Shandy (I, xix, 57-64), and the wounding of uncle Toby at the Battle of Namur (I, xxi; xxv, 75; 87). Upon closer examination, however, the connection, although often vague, can be deciphered.

In volume I, chapter xiv, for example, Tristram attempts to introduce his discussion of the midwife. Quickly, his attempted narration is halted with a seeming intrusion of the issue of his "mother's marriage settlement." Tristram, however, has a unique purpose in the intrusion, "in order to satisfy myself and the reader in a point necessary to be clear'd up, before we could proceed any further in this history" (I, xiv, 40). Because Tristram views the issues of childbearing, as outlined in the settlement, as crucial to the full appreciation of the story of the midwife, he chooses to relate this story, being reminded of its contents at mention of the midwife, before commencing with his narrative. Clearly, the stories, though seemingly unrelated, share a commonality in the issue of childbirth. This event illustrates Locke's theory of two seemingly unrelated ideas related in the mind as a result of its connection by a common factor, however far removed. The association of ideas is, as Locke notes, natural to the mind, in that "there is no one thing...which is not capable of almost an infinite number of considerations" (321). The mind does not link ideas which bear no resemblance. Although the events in *Tristram Shandy* seem unordered, therefore, they are indeed ordered in the most natural way possible. Thus, the representation of these ideas in the text, in Lockean terms, is both natural and necessary to the communication of Tristram's own particular associations.

According to Locke, the mind is, at all times, swimming with simultaneous and associated ideas: "'tis past doubt," Locke insists, "that Men have in their Minds several ideas" (104). More often than not, these ideas unite in the mind to form associations, such that several scattered ideas can meld into one distinct or central idea composed of an infinite number of components. This, Locke explains, comprises the natural order of the mind, "and whatever we can consider as one thing, whether a real Being, or Idea, suggests to the Understanding, the *Idea of Unity*" (131). Thus, although Sterne denies the conventional idea of Aristotelian unity, his work is, in fact, ordered. The novel illustrates, in fact, the union of several associated ideas into a whole. Although not a whole as Aristotle defines, it is, in relation to the mind, a whole in a Lockean and natural sense:

> Undoubtedly Sterne used the term ['digressive method'] because the normal expectation of his age (as of ours) was that plot, a chronology of events, shall be the scaffolding of fiction. Yet chronology is not the scaffolding of *Tristram Shandy*. [It is, however, an] organic structure emanating from the mind of the narrator, Tristram. (Cash, "The Lockean" 125)

Tristram Shandy, as a reflection of the continuous thought of its narrator, is a continuous story. Early in the novel, Tristram devotes himself to the lifelong pursuit of his work, insisting "I have constructed the main work and the adventitious parts of it with such intersections...one wheel within another, that the whole machine, in general, has been kept a-going;---and, what's more, it shall be kept a-going...so long with life and good spirits" (I, xxii, 81-2). Like his mind, and as a reflection of his mind, Tristram's story will continue for the duration of his own life. This is the natural order he has granted to his work. Freed from Aristotelian conventions and, as Benjamin H. Lehman notes in his essay *On Time, Personality, and the Author*, "under the dominance of its own laws...There is no selection and ordering...in terms of a falsifying line of action called a plot. The activity goes on, whether forward or backward, by the associational relevance of the apparently irrelevant" (27). Thus, as Watt states, "Sterne... can manipulate until we are giddy without any breach of narrative authenticity, since every transition is part of a hero's mental life which, of course, is very little concerned with chronological order" (305). Tristram's deconstruction of the conventional plot is justified here, due to the fact that the events of the story are related in a much more natural way than that of the linear and unified narrative.

Although it is a given that Tristram's story could easily have been told in a linear fashion, a truth of which "Sterne and the reader are always aware," chronology only applies to the "traditional novel." Tristram, in his attempt to portray "the inner reality, the full truth about how life and opinions are related to each other and to truth itself," must tell his story in such a way, in accordance with the natural order of his mind

(Cash, "The Lockean" 232). This natural order which entails the free association of observations and experiences are what grants Tristram insight into life's deepest truths, truths which, thus far, have been hidden and misrepresented by traditional thought.

Chapter 8:

Truth and Nature/ Nature and Truth

Locke insists that all truths are derived from a combination of experience and observation. In his *Epistle to the Reader*, Locke states that "every step the mind takes in its Progress towards knowledge, makes some Discovery, which is not only new, but the best too, for the time at least" (6). *Tristram Shandy*, essentially a series of "steps" in the formation of his autobiography, is an account of the narrator's experiences recovered from the memory, the "unfold[ing]" of which, according to Sterne in a statement on Lockean psychology, unfold, as well, "all the secrets of the mind; and shunning the errors to which other theories of knowledge are exposed, it arrives at all truths accessible to the understanding" (qtd. in McKillop 44). The experiences of both Walter and Tristram grant the characters valuable insights into the realities of nature, when their life-long plans become altered.

Although filled with digressions and improvisations, *Tristram Shandy* has a plan, although dissimilar to the far-fetched plans of Walter Shandy. Both Walter and Tristram come to realize, however, that plans and ordered events in any form are unreliable. Nature does not allow for a sure sequence of events, nor does it allow for determined endings. Walter Shandy, as evident upon many occasions, is an ordered man. With his monthly winding of the clock, his planned scheme for Tristram's future, and the ordered structure of his "*beds of justice*," Walter prepares so that his life will offer him no surprises (VI, xvi, 522). Yet, almost each plan Walter sets in motion is thwarted by unforeseen circumstance. Whether it is the incident of Tristram's nose, resulting from the very plan to ensure the proper delivery of the baby's brain (II, xix, 174-81), the incident of Tristram's mistaken naming (IV, xiv, 344), or the manner of his untimely circumcision (V, xvii, 449), Walter's plans almost inevitably result in tragedy. His displeasure upon these chance disruptions is ever-present:

> But how were we defeated!...when the few animal spirits I was worth in the world, and with which memory, fancy, and quick parts should have been convey'd,–were all dispersed, confused, confounded, scattered, and sent to the devil. (IV, xix, 354)

Here, Walter's linear plan becomes scattered, and, being of traditional mind, such circumstances confound him: "Had I faith in astrology, brother...I would have sworn some retrograde planet was hanging over this unfortunate house of mine, and turning every individual thing in it out of its place" (III, xxiii, 243). Finally, Walter questions his linear methods. If nature, as dictated by antiquity, exists in a complete and unified fashion, he wonders how it is possible that his unity has collapsed, and how it is possible that "with all my precautions...how was my system turned topside turvy in the womb with my child...that at this hour 'tis ninety *per Cent* insurance, that the fine network of the intellectual web be not rent and torn to a thousand tatters" (IV, xix, 355). What has been traditionally perceived as the natural order, namely, the linear sequence of time, has been misleading. Although evident in many of Tristram's earlier volumes, it is not until his own order is disrupted that he realizes the truth of this fact.

Upon the death of Bobby, Tristram curses the natural interruption of death upon the life of man, questioning, "what is the life of Man! Is it not to shift from side to side?—from sorrow to sorrow?—to button up one cause of vexation!—and unbutton another!" (IV, xxxi, 399). Upon further contemplation of death, and the causes of death, Tristram realizes that man may attempt to order life, but the natural order is that of the mind, with its many intersections, delineations and unforeseen intrusions:

> The two great causes, which conspire with each other to shorten life... are first—'The

internal spirit, which like a gentle flame, wastes the body down to death:—And secondly, the external air, that parches the body up to ashes:—which two enemies attacking us on both sides of our bodies together, at length destroy our organs, and render them unfit to carry on the functions of life. (V, xxxv, 473-74)

Never is this fact stressed most clearly upon Tristram than when he himself is faced with death, and the intrusive black page of Yorick threatens to descend upon his own story as it did upon that of the parson.

Prior to his illness, Tristram had a plan for his story "which I am resolved to follow;---and that is,---not to be in a hurry;---but to go on leisurely, writing and publishing two volumes of my life every year...[which] I shall continue to do as long as I live" (I, xiv, 42). Tristram resolves to "write full" and "free from cares...count[ing] not the number of my scars." Initially, Tristram is willing to follow the natural progress of time, allowing "my pen [to] take...its course...[to] write a careless kind of civil, non-sensical, good humoured *Shandean* book, which will do all your hearts good" (VI, xvii, 525). These plans are disrupted, and his leisurely attitude changes, however, upon the impending threat of death.

Suddenly, Tristram's narrative pace quickens when his plan to write until the end of his tale has been threatened: "Where am I? and into what a delicious riot of things am I rushing? I—I who must be cut short in the midst of my days, and taste no more of 'em than what I borrow from my imagination" (VII, xiv, 595). From here, Tristram begins his flight from death, his avoidance of nature. Trying to obtain all humanly experience in the time he has remaining, he "mak[es] all possible speed, from/*Ailly au Clochers*, I got to Hixcourt,/from Hixcourt, I got to Pequignay, and/from Pequignay, I got to Amiens" (VII, xv, 596). Contrary to the intricate detail granted to the previous incidents in his tale, suddenly, Tristram finds that he is pressed for time, and upon his minimal description of Paris, claims that "I cannot stop a moment to give you the character of the people—their genius—their manners—their customs...qualified as I may be" (VII, xix, 604). Tristram suddenly realizes that he has "forty volumes to write, and forty thousand things to say and do" in the time he has remaining, and against the threat of death, he chooses to "fly for [his] life" (VII, i, 576-7). It appears that suddenly the plan for his novel may be in jeopardy; suddenly his associational order may not ensure the completion of his tale, due to the endless associations of the mind which, "without being ever able to come to any stop or stint, let[s] us enlarge it as much as we will," defined by Locke as "the *Idea of Immensity*" (168). With this in mind, Tristram becomes reluctant to make promises in regards to the completion of his tale: "I take my leave of you," Tristram informs his readers, "till this time twelve-month, when (unless this vile cough kills me in the meantime) I'll have another pluck at your beards" (IV, xxxii, 402). Faced with his own mortality and the possibility of an incomplete autobiography, Tristram attempts a reorganization of his thoughts: a redirection from the associative order of the mind, to the traditional order of the unified plot.

Chapter 9:

And so it Be-ends...

Upon the conclusion of Volume VI, Tristram illustrates the visual representation of the progression of his work, thus far. In the illustrations, he maps the deviations from the traditions of linear narrative, and insists that from this point to the end of his tale, he is going to stick with this traditional method. "In this last volume," Tristram states, "I have done better still —for from the end of *Le Fever*'s episode, to the beginning of my uncle *Toby*'s campaigns,—I have scarce stepped a yard out of my way." Tristram, here, expresses a need to "mend" his writing at this point, in his desire to arrive at an ending through the linear narration of his tale in a *"right line."* This desire is significant. Visualizing the end of his life fast approaching, he incorporates into his text, the traditional order; thus, the "shortest line...which can be drawn from one given point to another...turning neither to the right hand or to the left" (VI, xl, 570-72), and ensuring, with greater probability, the conclusion of his tale. Tristram's experiences both in life and with death, however, as well as in his flight from death, has granted him the wisdom of nature, and most importantly, the conviction of the natural qualities of his own writing.

Tristram relates the story of Amandus and Amanda, "two fond lovers, separated from each other by cruel parents and by still more cruel destiny" who meet again by "chance" (VII, xxxi, 627-28). Tristram claims to have been deeply affected by this tale, having "afford[ed him] more *pabulum* to the brain, that all the *Frusts*, and *Crusts*, and *Rusts* of Antiquity which travelers can cook up for it" (VII, xxxi, 628). What the story has imparted on Tristram is the reality of nature, and upon traversing to the lovers' tomb to shed tears over their remains, when he arrives "there was no tomb to drop" his tear "upon" (VII, xl, 643). Thus, once again, Tristram's plan falls through. It is after this event, however, that Tristram decides to embrace chance, not run from it, to accept the impossibility of a determinate ending and abandon the linear order which his tale has adopted.

Once again, Tristram takes the leisurely route through his last days, resolving to "traverse upon my mule at my own leisure—*at my own leisure*—for I had left Death," and although death "still… followed," and although "I [still] fled him…I fled him cheerfully" (VII, xlii, 645). Although Tristram does not embrace death, he does accept the natural reality of chance, and of the possibility of an incomplete ending:

The sun was set-they had done their work; the

> nymphs had tied up their hair afresh...My mule made a dead point...I'll not go a step further—'Tis very well, Sir, said I—I never will argue a point with one of your family, as long as I live. (VII, xliii, 649)

Experience also reveals to Tristram the reality of nature, that life, at any time can be interrupted. Recalling the initial sexual relations of Toby and the widow Wadman, Tristram "call[s] all the powers of time and chance, which severely check us in our careers in this world, to bear me witness, that I could never yet get fairly to my uncle Toby's amours, 'till this very moment, that my mother's *curiosity*...wished her to take a peep at them through the key-hole" (IX, i, 735). As chance causes for the untimely interruption of the love-making of uncle Toby and widow Wadman, so too does it impede on Tristram's own story. Moreover, as a result of his acceptance of this fact, Tristram offers his tale, on the chance of its incompletion, to anyone who wishes to offer it resolution, "for though I have all along been hastening towards this part of it...any one is welcome to take my pen, and go on with the story for me that will...I have still some hopes of remaining...[though] be it which it will...I leave the affair entirely to the *invoked*, to inspire or to inject me according as he sees good" (IX, xxiv, 779). Tristram now accepts the unpredictability of life, and finds as well, new meaning and appreciation for his own work.

Conclusion:

The Story of a "Cock and a Bull..."

Classical literature, in its ruled order of events, constitutes an unjust imitation of nature. Although reputed as the most precise imitation of nature, Tristram now realizes that life cannot be defined by planned plots and ordered events. Moreover, the order it has imposed upon literature is now revealed to have been based on the false premise of perfect natural imitation. Life's true representation is in the process of the mind, and in the interruptions of thought and consciousness which reflect the chance circumstance of nature:

> O ye water-drinkers! Is it then by this delusive fountain, that ye have so often governed and turned this world about like a mill-wheel—grinding the faces of the impotent—be-powdering their ribs—be-peppering their noses, and changing sometimes even the very frame and face of nature. (VIII, v, 661)

As a result of the classical misrepresentation of nature, Tristram finds invigorated meaning and value in his own work, and "for my own part, I am resolved never to read any book but my own, as long as I live" (661). Furthermore, Tristram expresses the "will...that all mankind should write as well as myself.–Which they certainly will, when they think as little" (IX, xii, 762). Good writing, thus, is not a matter of intellectual planning, but simply a matter of writing one's own mind and experiences in natural, as opposed to contrived, progressions, as McKeon reiterates:

> The unities of time and place entail the ideal of a precise correspondence between the circumstantial conditions of the events that are fictionally depicted and those that govern their actual depiction. And to understand both the unities and the claim to historicity we must look not to classical authority but to the empirical revolution. (127)

Tristram now realizes that his story, complete with all of its digressions and interruptions, is the true representation of nature, as Lehman insists, "like nature," Tristram's story "does not begin anywhere or end anywhere, or perhaps we should say it does begin anywhere and end anywhere" (31). The conclusion of Tristram's tale is proof of this conviction. Obadiah's failure to predict the date of his Bull's "calving," suggesting "she'll calve on Monday–on Tuesday–on Wednesday at the farthest," is a natural example of the failure to derive absolute chronological predictions in nature. Walter attempts to suggest a possible conclusion to the tale, namely, that "the cow [may] be barren?," when Elizabeth symbolically interjects, and when inquiring "what is all this story about?," Yorick famously replies, "A COCK and a BULL... and one of the best of its kind I ever heard" (IX, xxxiii, 807-9). For Yorick, the tale is complete. Unsurity is as close to completion as nature will allow man to traverse. Life, reminiscent of the story, is a "Cock" and "Bull" story, a non-sensical tale filled with the circumstance and miscalculations inherent in nature:

> For Sterne, the world is contingency incarnate. Anything and everything may be upset by thoroughly but irrelevantly motivated chance. If chance sometimes advances a clean line of action, it more often impedes it or carries it on a tangent. (Lehman 24)

As Lehman further insists, this improbability is the "stark reality of the world...[thus] Sterne's intelligence made nonsense of [life]...since it could not make sense" (25). As a result of this realization, Sterne, through the construct of *Tristram Shandy*, deconstructs the powerful hold which antiquity has, throughout history, maintained over literary society. In a significant step towards the evolution of the modern novel, Sterne defines his place in literature as the author who redefined the truthful representation of nature inherent within all men.

In *The Life and Opinions of Tristram Shandy, Gentleman*, Laurence Sterne claims to be limited by no traditional order. As such, the work is fragmented and scattered. It is ordered not in the sequence of time, nor in the tradition of a unified plot, but in the sequence of thought. A demonstration of Lockean psychology, it is a novel which represents the order, not of convention but the order of the mind, specifically, the order of Tristram's mind, who, in true Lockean form, relates events and recollections as they occur to him. His story is driven, not by linearity, but by association, and by the train of thought which enables the story as it enables Tristram's pen. John Locke's *Essay Concerning Human Understanding*, in this way, serves as the foundation upon which Sterne achieves literary independence. In his narrative, he follows the new natural human order defined by Locke in the treatise, the order which allows him not only to enact the evolution of the narrative method, but to discover the truth inherent in himself, the truth about life which he entails from his experiences and recollections: namely, that life, like his story, is unpredictable. Like the mind, life is not based on rules and guidelines, but on chance and association, driven by an endless chain of circumstance. As such, the traditional Aristotelian order proves not only, in the opinion of Tristram, to be confined, but also to be a falsified representation of life, which is not ordered or predetermined, and which does not, as the traditional novel insists, have a determined conclusion. *Tristram Shandy* is, in essence a satire on life. Like the narrative itself, life is merely a "cock" and "bull" story, which cannot be ordered by any formal structure.

Appendix

Kidgell, John. *The card...* Vol. 1. London, [1755]. *Eighteenth Century Collections Online*. Web. 18 Oct. 2013. P. 12.

THE CARD.

the *Evelyns* retract the Refolution which they had formed of *Archibald*'s compleating the intended *Tour*. They feared the Cenfure of the World, upon a Return premature and abrupt, and came to an immediate Determination, to make the defigned Propofal to Dr. *Elwes*. Sir *James* therefore faid, he would *wait upon* the *Doctor*, to confer with him inftantly; but the Ladies, (for Reafons of no impenetrable Curiofity) thought it more convenient to *send for* him. They were fure the Doctor would be fo obliging as to come with Pleafure, and for Sir *James* to go, would be but Fatigue and Inconvenience. In Confequence of this Decifion, Mifs *Evelyn* obtained the Favour of *the ten of Clubs*, to wait upon Doctor *Elwes*, on the fairer Side of which, (etched in beautiful Manufcript) was this important Commiffion.

Page 12.

..., and Lady Evelyn's Com—
...ts to M.r Clives hope He
...ght no Cold in the Journey
...d beg the favour of his Company
...t Evelyn Hall immediately if
...convenient — tuesday 11 o Clock.

Works Cited

Anderson, Howard ed. *Tristram Shandy*. By Laurence Sterne. New York: Norton, 1980.

Aristotle. *Poetics.* Trans. Malcolm Heath. New York: Penguin, 1996.

Braudy, Leo. "The Form of the Sentimental Novel." *Novel* 7 (Autumn 1973): 5-13.

Brumwell, Stephen and W. A. Speck. *Cassell's Companion to Eighteenth-Century Britain*. Ed. Derek Beales. New York: Cassell, 2001.

Campbell, Duncan. *The Beautiful Oblique: Conceptions of Temporality in 'Tristram Shandy.'* Oxford: P. Lang, 2002.

Cash, Arthur H. *Laurence Sterne: The Early and Middle Years*. London: Methuen, 1975.

---. "The Lockean Psychology of *Tristram Shandy*." *ELH* 22 (June 1955): 125-35.

Gardiner, Juliet ed. *The History Today: Who's Who in British History*. London: Collins & Brown, 2000.

Johnson, Samuel. "The Rambler no. 4." *The Yale Edition of the Works of Samuel Johnson Vol. III*. Ed. W. J. Bate and Albrecht B. Strauss. New Haven: Yale UP, 1969. 19-25.

Keymer, Tom. *Sterne, the Moderns, and the*

Novel. Toronto: Oxford UP, 2002.

Kidgell, John. *The card...* Vol. 1. London, [1755]. *Eighteenth Century Collections Online*. Web. 18 Oct. 2013. P. 12.

Lehman, Benjamin H. "Of Time, Personality, and the Author." *Laurence Sterne: A Collection of Critical Essays*. Ed. John Traugott. Englewood Cliffs: Prentice-Hall, 1968. 21-33.

Locke, John. *An Essay Concerning Human Understanding*. Ed. Peter H. Nidditch. Oxford: Clarendon, 1975.

Macrone, Michael. *It's Greek to Me!* New York: Cader, 1991.

McKeon, Michael. *The Origins of the English Novel: 1600-1740*. Baltimore: Johns Hopkins UP, 1987.

McKillop, Alan Dugald. "Laurence Sterne." *Laurence Sterne: A Collection of Critical Essays*. Ed. John Traugott. Englewood Cliffs: Prentice-Hall, 1968. 34-65.

New, Melvyn and Joan New ed. *The Florida Edition of the Works of Laurence Sterne: The Life and Opinions of Tristram Shandy, Gentleman.* By Laurence Sterne. Gainesville: UP of Florida, 1978

Pfister, Manfred. *Laurence Sterne*. Tavistock: Northcote, 2001.

Ress, Laura Jane. "The Sentimental Novel and

Tristram Shandy." Tender Consciousness: Sentimental Sensibility in the Emerging Artist. New York: P. Lang, 2002.

Ross, Ian Campbell. *Laurence Sterne: A Life*. New York: OUP, 2001.

Simon, Irène ed. *Neo-Classical Criticism: 1600-1800.* London: Edward Arnold, 1971.

Sterne, Laurence. *The Florida Edition of the Works of Laurence Sterne: The Life and Opinions of Tristram Shandy, Gentleman.* Ed. Melvyn New and Joan New. Gainesville: UP of Florida, 1978.

Watt, Ian P. *The Rise of the Novel; Studies in Defoe, Richardson, and Fielding.* Berkeley: U of California P, 1967.

Woolf, Virginia. *The Common Reader: Second Series.* London: Hogarth, 1948.

Problematic Press is a small, independent book publishing endeavour based in St. John's, NL. Problematic Press has a mission with a broad scope, aiming to entertain and educate readers of all ages.

Perhaps that's problematic.

Problems make us think.

http://problematicpress.wordpress.com

www.ingramcontent.com/pod-product-compliance
Lightning Source LLC
Chambersburg PA
CBHW071414040426
42444CB00009B/2251